THE OLD TESTAMENT
AND JESUS CHRIST

THE OLD TESTAMENT AND JESUS CHRIST

By Claus Westermann

Translated by
Omar Kaste

AUGSBURG PUBLISHING HOUSE
Minneapolis, Minnesota

THE OLD TESTAMENT AND JESUS CHRIST

This volume is a translation of *Das Alte Testament und Jesus Christus*, published in 1968 by Calwer Verlag, Stuttgart, Germany.

Contents

Changed View of Relation Between the Testaments

The Old Testament was the Bible of early Christianity. The New Testament writings came to be part of the Bible only because they were joined to the Old Testament. For the earliest Christians Holy Scripture was a known and established quantity; what had been Scripture for Jesus of Nazareth was to continue to be Scripture also for the early Christian church. Because they contained the words and works of the God by whom Jesus knew himself to have been sent, and whom he addressed as Father, the Old Testament Scriptures were for Christians inseparable from Jesus' own words and works. For the first Christians, this close identification of Jesus' words and actions with the words and works of God as they are presented in the Old Testament was a fundamental and unquestioned prerequisite of their own existence.

It is not surprising, then, that the New Testament's proclamation of Jesus as the Christ consistently relies

on the Old Testament. This is reflected in the large
number of Old Testament quotations which are contained in all New Testament writings and which constitute a considerable part of them. It can also be seen
in an abundance of associations, not always readily
recognizable, in the New Testament's language: figures of speech, images, names for people and things,
and collective and individual patterns for worship and
everyday life.

The New Testament's proclamation of Jesus Christ
is founded on the Old Testament. Just what this means
for the church, for her message and activity, has been
seen and judged in many different ways in the course
of her history. Stated radically, the question is whether
or not this Old Testament-relatedness of the message
about Christ extends to the very center of Christian
doctrine and teaching, to its witness to Christ. Ever
since Marcion, there have been those within the church
who, for the sake of "pure doctrine," have demanded a
separation of the Christian message from the Old
Testament. They contrast the God of the Old Testament with the New Testament God, and criticize the
Old Testament itself as a record of an alien religion.

These voices, however, have never been able to gain
the upper hand in the church. Down to the present
the Old Testament has remained a part of the Bible of
all Christian churches, and the church has continued
to hold that the doctrine of Jesus Christ can only be
grounded in the Old Testament. However, even among
those who have held fast to this conviction, there have

been widely differing methods of expressing and applying it. They have ranged from total adaptation of the Gospel of Jesus Christ to agree with the Old Testament to a total adaptation of the Old Testament to fit the Gospel.

The uncertainty about this question has continued down to the present and results mainly from the fact that the relation between the Old Testament and Christ's doctrine has been understood as the relation between individual passages in the two Testaments. That is, beginning with a single Old Testament text, one attempted to determine its relationship to a single passage in the New Testament. For example, the passage in Genesis 3:15, "He [the seed of the woman] shall bruise your head...," was interpreted as a reference to the victory of Christ over Satan (the serpent). The passage in Isaiah 7:14, "Behold, a young woman shall conceive and bear a son...," was understood to refer to the Virgin Mary and the birth of Jesus. In Isaiah 6:3, "Holy, holy, holy is the Lord of hosts," the threefold repetition of "holy" was said to refer to the Trinity.

Plainly, such interpretation based on comparison of isolated texts brings a strong factor of unreliability into the attempt to determine the Old Testament's relation to the message about Christ. This determination depends upon the interpretation of single statements without regard to their context. Moreover, the understanding of these Old Testament texts can change, especially when they are random passages unrelated to one another.

The practice of relating the Christian message to isolated passages in the Old Testament has played an important role in the Christian church because the same thing is done in the New Testament. In the Gospels and Epistles, isolated Old Testament passages often are related to Christ or to the church without regard to the context from which they come. The significance and meaning of such passages are largely independent of their original context. Yet this signified no unreliability for the New Testament, because the unity of the Old Testament was so supremely unaffected by anything outside of itself that no examination of its contexts was necessary, and because the fundamental importance of the Old Testament for the message of Christ was so taken for granted that it did not need to be supported by proof passages.

Now, however, some changes have taken place. Our understanding of the Scriptures has changed, as have our use and interpretation of Scripture. These changes have not happened just within the church or within theological study, but are a product of the total spiritual and intellectual climate, apart from which the church and theology cannot exist.

Two transformations, especially, have been of substantial importance in determining the relation of the Old Testament Scriptures to that which has happened through Christ.

We have come to see the importance of context in understanding both the Old and New Testaments. We recognize that each passage must be understood in terms of what precedes and follows it. Any interpretation of an isolated statement which ignores the context of that passage can no longer expect general acceptance. This applies also to the understanding of an Old Testament passage which is quoted in the New Testament: Though we may recognize that its interpretation, based on the completely different hermeneutic principles of its day, may still make sense in the place where it is cited, we can no longer understand it in just the same way. Today anyone who has to do with biblical interpretation knows that he can hope to find listeners only when he takes into consideration that the key to the understanding of any particular passage is its context.

The second change consists in the fact that we now understand that the words of the Bible cannot be viewed on the same historical level. It is generally recognized that the biblical books represent a historical narrative, and that they came into being in the course of the events they describe. This fact has its application when the proclamation about Christ is related to the Old Testament. The relation of any Old Testament passage to Christ must be a historical one, for each statement was made on an occasion along the way which led from Abraham to Christ. Because it arose in a specific situation, the Old Testament passage has a historical context which must always be taken into consideration, whether it has a direct effect on the interpretation of the passage or not.

When the Old Testament came to be understood

in context and in historical sequence, it was no longer possible to contrast the content of the Testaments in such a way, for instance, as to say that "the Old Testament speaks of an angry God, but the New Testament deals with God's grace"; or, "The Old Testament represents the Law, but the New Testament is Gospel"; or, "The salvation of the Old Testament has to do with earthly goods, while in the New Testament the term refers to spiritual blessings." Nor could even such fundamentally correct descriptions of the content of the Testaments as "promise" and "fulfillment" be used any longer in a generalized way to describe their relation to one another, as if the entire Old Testament consisted of "promise" and the entire New Testament of "fulfillment."

With this viewing of Old Testament passages in their contexts came also a change in the understanding of so-called "scriptural proof." It is now recognized that when something reported in the New Testament is authenticated by citing an Old Testament passage introduced by the formula, "This came to pass in order to fulfill that which was written . . . ," this demonstrated to those who heard this statement that what was happening in Christ was anchored in the Scriptures. This formula says nothing about the significance of the passage in its original setting, or about the meaning it had for those to whom it was first directed. We must, therefore, limit the meaning of "scriptural proof" to the special function it had within the limits of the scriptural understanding of New Testament times. It is not possible to demonstrate that Jesus is the Christ by citing a random passage in the Old Testament, at least not in such a way as to make faith in Jesus as the Christ either easier or unnecessary. This is reflected today in the conversations between the Christian church and Judaism; at no time do its participants conduct this discussion in such a way as to ask if isolated Old Testament passages prove that Jesus is the Christ or not. It is understood that only by emphasizing the larger contexts of both Testaments can this conservation be conducted.

Today our understanding of the relation of the Testaments to each other has changed from what it was during earlier periods of the church's history, such as the Reformation era; in fact, we often cannot duplicate even the New Testament's manner of understanding and using Old Testament passages. The real reason for this changed point of view must be sought in God's activity apart from his people and outside of the Christian church.

As the Creator, God remains Lord of creation and Lord of human history. Changes such as the shift from a pre-historical to a historical way of thinking, which have affected our understanding and interpretation of the Bible, have not happened independently of God, any more than has the shift to better understanding of the natural sciences, an understanding which directly affects the conditions of man's existence. When we inquire about the meaning of these great transformations which affect the history of humanity, our

questioning is grounded in an affirmation of God as
the Lord of creation and of human history.

The Old Testament
and Jesus Christ

In investigating the relation of the Old Testament
to the proclamation about Christ, we must first consider its primary organization into books of history,
books of prophecy, and writings. Before we under-
take this, however, we shall turn to an Old Testament
book in which these three principal kinds of material,
though intimately related to one another, point beyond
themselves to something new. This is the book of the
prophet Second Isaiah, the prophet of the Babylonian
exile. His message combines prophecy with the history
of the people of God and their response in lament and
praise.

Second Isaiah, the last of the prophets in the pre-
exile tradition, announces deliverance and a new beginning for the defeated and exiled people. The servant
of God passages in Second Isaiah announce the ap-
pearance of something entirely new, something un-
known in the entire Old Testament until that time:
the possibility of a new existence founded on the
atoning suffering of one individual (Isaiah 53). Whether the expiatory suffering and death of the servant of
God is an event in the past, present, or future is not
specified. The cancellation of people's sins through
the servant of God refers to an event which cannot be

shown to refer clearly to any other happening in the Old Testament. The New Testament's identification of this servant of God with Christ is perfectly valid. The parallel between the acts of the servant of God, who, though he suffers and dies, receives God's approval in spite of death or because of it, is the most obvious contact between the Old Testament and the New Testament's description of Jesus Christ. The parallel between the servant of God in Isaiah 42:1-4; 49:1-6; 50:4-9; 52:13—53:12, and the figure of Jesus Christ is commented upon in approximately 17 New Testament passages. Among these passages are Isaiah 42:1-4, in Matthew 12:18-21 and Isaiah 53 in 1 Peter 2:21-25.

Contemporary scholars recognize this just as fully as did the early Christians, and it is acknowledged by many Jewish theologians. Consequently, we are on sure ground at this point, and a secure point of departure is that the proclamation of the message of Christ is rooted in the figure of the servant of God.

Nevertheless, what is said about the servant of God in these passages is not exclusively meant as a forecast or prediction. Rather, it is a message directed to those living in the prophet's own time. This is shown most clearly in that part of Isaiah 53 in which the chorus of those affected by the suffering and death of the servant of God confess that they had at first misunderstood this new act of God, that is that they had thought the servant of God was suffering the punishment for his own sins: "Yet we esteemed him stricken, smitten by God, and afflicted..." (Isaiah 53:1-6).

Here we see that this new reality required a transformation in the thinking of the people of that time. The suffering of the servant of God belongs in a series of events in which it signified a basic turning-point. Thus, the servant of God passages can be understood only in relation to these events, never as predictions of Christ without context, which could have been found in any part of the Old Testament. The servant of God passages belong, first of all, in the context of Second Isaiah's prophecy and thus in the history of the prophets in general. We must ask what meaning they have in and for the history of prophecy.

The relation of Second Isaiah's message to the historical books is established by the prophet's comparison of Israel's salvation from exile, which he is announcing, to its initial deliverance from oppression in Egypt. The narrative of the historical books begins with this first exodus from Egypt, and now Second Isaiah announces a second exodus. For Second Isaiah, the history of Israel begins with its having been saved at the beginning of its history and extends to the deliverance from Babylon, which he is promising. This corresponds to the span of time covered by the historical books of the Old Testament.

There is also a clear connection with the Writings, the third part of the Old Testament. More than any prophet before him, Second Isaiah brought his message into a close relation with the prayers of complaint (lament) and the prayers of praise, the basic elements of the Psalter. His promise of redemption is an answer to the complaints of the suffering people of God in exile, and those who hear this promise, anticipating its fulfillment, respond with praise of God.

The prophecy of Second Isaiah in the servant of God passages has a position of key importance in the Old Testament. At that time in the history of God's people, his words clearly expressed the interdependence and unity of prophecy, national history, and the people's response to God's acts through their praise and prayers for deliverance. It is not accidental that at precisely this key point in the servant of God passages the relation of the message about Christ to the Old Testament is clearest and most unequivocal.

Chapter One

Old Testament's Prophetic Message and Jesus Christ

The Lament of the Prophets

The servant of God passages, as has been noted, must be considered first in the context of Second Isaiah's prophecy, and also in the context of the whole history of the prophets. In one of the servant of God passages, Isaiah 49:1-6, specific reference is made to the life of the prophets. Here the prophet complains that his efforts to bring Israel back to God have been in vain. In spite of this lament, however, he is given an expanded task: "I will give you as a light to the nations" (Isaiah 49:6). The lament of the servant alludes to the history of the prophets, especially to the apparently fruitless efforts of the prophets of judgment before the exile. The servant of God knows that he stands in the tradition of the prophets, even though he himself is no longer only a prophet. Something new is revealed in his expanded task: His service is no longer to be limited to Israel, for God has chosen him to be a light to all nations. When in the New Testament these words are applied to Christ (Luke 2:32; Acts 13:47), this is in harmony with the actual meaning of the servant of God passage.

The complaint of the servant that he has tried vainly to bring Israel back to God (Isaiah 49:4) reports a state of affairs to which the prophetic books testify in many ways, namely, that the efforts of the prophets to bring their people back to God apparently had been fruitless. Successes are not reported for a single one of them. The message of judgment of every pre-exile prophet from Amos through Jeremiah seems to go completely unheeded, powerless to affect the history of the nation.

For the prophets, this meant that their task brought them suffering. This suffering is most forcefully expressed in the prophecy of Jeremiah, where it becomes an essential part of the prophetic office. The activity of Jeremiah is not greatly separated in time from that of Second Isaiah. Jeremiah prophesied immediately before the beginning of the exile in 587 B.C., Second Isaiah shortly thereafter. In the Book of Jeremiah the suffering of the prophet as a result of his task is expressed in a variety of forms. Again and again in the announcements of judgment which the prophet is commanded to speak we find statements in which Jeremiah movingly says how he suffers with the people and sorrows because of the catastrophe which threatens them (for example, Jeremiah 4:19; 8:18-23). Corresponding to this is the lament of God himself who suffers because of the judgment he must bring down upon his own people. In one important part of the Book of Jeremiah, Baruch, Jeremiah's comrade, tells the story of Jeremiah's suffering. Running like a thread throughout Baruch's account is his statement that the message of Jeremiah encountered rejection and recalcitrance, that the prophet was increasingly subjected to hostility and persecution, prevented from exercising his office, threatened with death, and deprived of his freedom. Suffering became part of his service. Finally, in the gripping lamentations (11:18–12:6; 15:10-20; 17:14-18; 18:18-23; 20:7-11; 20:14-18), Jeremiah himself speaks out his sorrow and desperation in the face of work which was becoming inhumanly difficult.

These lamentations, unique in the prophetic books, are the most definite preparation for the suffering of the servant of God in Second Isaiah. Yet there is one important difference: unlike Second Isaiah, Jeremiah could see no positive purpose in the sorrow which came to him because of his calling. The vicarious, atoning suffering of the servant of God in Second Isaiah was something entirely new and unprecedented, and yet a clearly discernible progression leads from the suffering of Jeremiah to the suffering of the servant of God. And so it becomes clear that in this particular aspect of the history of the prophets, the suffering of the one whom God has charged with responsibility for his people, there was a goal which later found historical fulfillment in Jesus Christ.

The Prophets as Messengers of Judgment

The relationship between the history of the prophets and Jesus Christ is different than ordinarily supposed. In some passages of the New Testament this connection is understood as if the prophets had foreseen that Christ would come, or that they had promised the coming of the Messiah. If that were the essential and decisive connection between the prophets and Christ, then it would have had nothing to do with the most important task of these prophets, which was to bring the message of judgment to their people. The prophets' promise of Christ would then have been only something which they had said in addition to their authentic message. It would have had no connection with the prophecy of judgment, for the sake of which the books of prophecy have been handed down to us.

However, the similarity between Jeremiah's suffering and the suffering of the servant of God reveals a common cause: the prophets' preaching of judgment. When in the servant of God passage (Isaiah 49:4) the servant states that his efforts to bring Israel back to God had been in vain, he is referring to the preaching of judgment which he shared with other pre-exile prophets. Jeremiah, too, suffers increasingly as he announces the coming of judgment.

The history of the prophets of judgment in Israel is intertwined with the history of the kingdom. We encounter it for the first time during the reign of King David (Nathan, Gad); Jeremiah, the last of the pre-

exile prophets, prophesied during the reign of Zedekiah, the last king of Judah. This contemporaneousness
of prophet and king is also important for the relation
to Christ, since the lines of succession of both the
prophets and the kings lead to him. During the first
period in the history of judgment prophecy, which
we know from the historical books of the Old Testament, God's judgment was proclaimed on individuals,
especially on kings; during the second period, that of
the prophetical books from Amos to Jeremiah and Ezekiel, his judgment was proclaimed upon the entire
nation. This preaching of judgment became necessary
because God's people then were in danger of separating
themselves from him by their disobedience, a step
which would have meant their destruction.

Seen in this light, even the announcement of the
coming judgment of God on his people had the protec-
tive purpose of "bringing Israel back to God." The
preaching of judgment by the prophets did not become
necessary because of individual sins, but rather because
a mountain of guilt had accumulated in the course of
Israel's history. The real threat to Israel's life was this
mountain of guilt and not her political enemies. When
Israel failed to acknowledge the guilt and to bear it,
judgment became inevitable. Only through forgiveness
was salvation possible, and that only for a remnant
(Isaiah 43:22-28; 40:2). The Old Testament, in passages such as that concerning the new Covenant in
Jeremiah 31:31-34, and the servant of God passage in
Isaiah 53, only hints that this forgiveness would come

about through entirely new divine action. Yet the judgment announcement of the prophets points toward this new event.

The Prophets as Messengers of Salvation

At no time were the prophets exclusively messengers of judgment. Because they were God's heralds, they were always, in some of their activities, messengers of redemption as well. But the prophetic message of salvation varied as much as the situations in which the prophets spoke. Amos had almost nothing to say about salvation; Isaiah was a prophet of judgment who proclaimed deliverance at certain times; Second Isaiah was exclusively a prophet of salvation. It follows from this that their messages of salvation referred to the near future of those to whom they spoke, not to the distant future.

The task of the prophets never consisted of predicting anything; that is a basic misunderstanding of prophecy, often understood as something predicted in ancient times which, after centuries, came true. Such foretelling or predicting can exist, but it has nothing to do with prophecy. An essential quality of a prophetic proclamation was its relationship to the people to whom the prophet addressed himself. In his prophecy, the prophet said something, whether it was a message of judgment or deliverance, to his contemporaries. It was something which made sense for them in their setting, and which applied to their future. Therefore, when we inquire about the relation to Christ of the prophets' announcements of salvation, we can never disregard the people to whom the announcements were made. Only by considering the people's history can any relation at all be established between an Old Testament passage and Christ.

If we want to affirm the Reformers' insistence on the plain sense of Scripture, we also cannot retreat to the possibility that such a prophetic passage had both an obvious meaning for the men to whom it was spoken and an esoteric meaning which did not reveal itself until it was fulfilled in Christ. Just as Jesus Christ was truly man, so the history of which he was the goal is real, finite history, and we have to treat it as such. We cannot expect to encounter among the Old Testament's numerous statements about salvation any prophecies of Christ which are independent of history — that is, prophecies in the sense of simple predictions.

To be sure, we will find statements about salvation which show a way to Christ through the history of God's people. But here again, it is in the context of the history of the promises and announcements of deliverance that we must look for a connection between these same promises and Christ.

The many statements about salvation in the Old Testament can be divided into three types: the promise of salvation, the proclamation of salvation, and the description of salvation.

Characteristic of the promise of salvation is that in a time of hopeless trouble and defeat it proclaims with authority: "God has had mercy on you; he has decreed a turning point for your trouble." It was a promise of salvation which went out to the Israelites during their oppression in Egypt: "I ... have heard their cries ..." (Exodus 3:7 ff.). The promise of salvation is also the form of the salvation statement which Second Isaiah speaks to the Israelites in the Babylonian exile: "Fear not, for I have redeemed you ..." (Isaiah 43:1). Here, as in the first example, full, complete, and inclusive deliverance is promised as already having been decided by God and set into motion. However, never do we find any example of promises of salvation which have to do directly with Christ.

Nonetheless, we probably will recognize the progression which begins with the promise of deliverance given to Israel in Egypt, the promise which initiated Israel's history, continues in the promise of salvation in the Babylonian Exile, and culminates in the New Testament proclamation of the coming of Christ and the coming of the kingdom of God. All contain a message about salvation; in all, salvation is proclaimed in such a way that when the announcement is made ("To you is born this day ... a Savior"), the coming of Christ means that the kingdom has already dawned. In all three cases it was through God's merciful turning to his people that deliverance came. In the case of his turning to Israel in Egypt, it was simply compassion on those who were suffering; in the case of Israel in the Babylonian exile, forgiveness was the basis of his merciful action. The new aspect of God's saving work in Christ was that God's mercy was no longer a reality for an entire nation, but only for those who affirmed his saving act in Christ.

The announcement of salvation concerned a single event through which God turned away trouble, freed from distress, or broke into a succession of events. In the Old Testament these announcements of salvation are always related to some particular turning point in the history of God's people, never to the coming of Jesus Christ.

The announcement of salvation was often associated with the promise of salvation. Along with the assurance that God had heard their cries and had had mercy on them, the prophet announced to Israel that God would bring them into a good land. Along with the assurance to Israel during the exile that God had forgiven their guilt and redeemed them, they also received the news of the marvelous return through the wilderness and the re-establishment of their homeland. In spite of the desperate situation in beleaguered Jerusalem, the prophet Jeremiah was commanded to make this announcement of salvation: "Houses and fields and vineyards shall again be bought in this land" (Jeremiah 32:15). On two occasions when the city was being threatened by its enemies, Isaiah announced in Jerusalem that it would be freed from the danger.

Often this kind of announcement of salvation was accompanied by a sign, as, for example, in Isaiah 7:7 when, as an enemy army drew near, the prophet told King Ahaz: "It [the plan to conquer Jerusalem] shall not stand and it shall not come to pass." The prophet offered the king a sign to confirm this statement, and when he refused it, the prophet said that God himself would give this sign: "Behold, a young woman shall conceive and bear a son, and shall call his name Immanuel" (Isaiah 7:14). The saving act of God proclaimed here was not the birth of the child, but the preservation of Jerusalem from its enemies. The name given to the child to be born would be the sign which confirmed this act of deliverance. The name of the child, Immanuel, that is, "God with us," reflected the thankful joy at the preservation of Jerusalem. Who the mother and the child were is neither stated nor hinted; this detail is not essential, for the naming of the child was the sign which promised that Jerusalem would be preserved. Both the proclamation of salvation and the sign which confirmed it had to do with an event which happened soon after the statement was made.

It was in this way that proclamation of salvation accompanied the steps of God's people. Their purpose was to tell those paralyzed by anxiety and desperation not to give up hope, to assure them that God's saving acts could make a future possible, in spite of the disasters which threatened. This is because these proclamations of salvation kept God's people on their course and made it possible for them to continue on it. These announcements, however, had no direct relation to Christ; they were not intended to be predictions of Christ; not even in retrospect can they be so inter-

preted. Among the great number of salvation announcements there are some, however, which allow us to
sense something new, something which points beyond
the Old Testament history of God's people.

In a word of judgment on the "scoffers who rule this
people in Jerusalem" (Isaiah 28:14-22), Isaiah says
something which directs our attention beyond the announcement of annihilation to a different kind of act
of God: "Behold I am laying in Zion for a foundation
a stone, a tested stone, a precious cornerstone, of a sure
foundation: 'He who believes will not be in haste.'"

This is not an announcement like that in Isaiah 7,
which says that Jerusalem will be saved from its enemies. On the contrary, God will carry through his
"alien work" of judgment among his own people, and
then he will begin an entirely new work. Zion, the
center of the people of God, will be re-established, and
faith will become the basis for belonging to God and
to his enterprise.

When this passage is interpreted in the New Testament to imply that Isaiah, in referring to the "cornerstone," had meant Christ (1 Peter 2:4-6), it is, of course,
reading more into the passage than it really intends.
The laying of the cornerstone meant the establishment
of God's people on a new foundation, nothing more.
To be sure, linking this passage with God's new work
is fitting in the sense that men's belonging to him is
founded on faith.

Another announcement of salvation which points
beyond the ancient people of God is found in Jeremiah

31:31-34. Here God reveals that he will make a new covenant with his people, one entirely different from the covenant Israel broke through its disobedience. These words, too, are correctly cited in the New Testament in relation to Christ, even though some things which they say refer to events as yet unfulfilled.

At any rate, these and many other announcements of salvation point beyond the history of the ancient people of God to something new which will come after the judgment. But not even these promises of deliverance specifically refer to Jesus.

The description of salvation is a form rooted, not in the words of the prophets, but in the ancient words of blessing and in the words of seers who described the future. The salvation description does not announce coming events; rather, it contrasts, in broad terms, the future with that of the present — in a period of blessedness beyond the present age everything will be different. Characteristic of the description is that the future salvation will extend also to the heathen and to all creation, and that its particular characteristics will be blessedness and peace.

The description of salvation is not directly related to Christ, and it can be so understood that it would be impossible to say that the deliverance it describes had been realized with the coming of Christ. When, for example, salvation is described in Isaiah 2:1-4 as a universal reign of peace and a pilgrimage of all peoples to Zion at a time when Mt. Zion appears as the center of the world, this vision of the future cannot be considered as having been fulfilled in the New Testament.

However, a certain group of salvation descriptions have, from earliest Christian times, played a special role in relating the Old Testament to Christ. These are the so-called messianic prophecies: Isaiah 4:2-6; 9:1-6; 11:1-9; 16:5; 32:1-8; Jeremiah 17:24-27; 23:5 ff.; 30:9, 21; 33:17; Ezekiel 17:22-24; 34:23 ff.; 37:22-25; Hosea 3:4; Amos 9:11; Micah 4:8; 5:1-3; Zechariah 9:9 ff. In these passages future salvation is conceived of as going out from a king who rules in an era of salvation, a king of blessing. He would be a descendant of the house of David, and a godly and righteous king: his reign would be a reign of peace. Even the animals would live together in peace, and through him the land would be blessed (Isaiah 11:1-10).

The reason these messianic promises have, from earliest Christian times down to the present, played such a pronounced role, especially in the church's Christmas carols, is to be found in a trait common to all of them: Never is it said of this coming king of salvation that he will conquer his kingdom, or that he will become king by means of some historical act. Rather, he will be born a king, and even the announcement of his birth will mean that the time of salvation has dawned (Isaiah 9:1-6). The birth of the Messiah or king of salvation will be the dawn of the new era. Nowhere is anything said about any historical activity of this king; he is to be a mediator through whom a new state of blessing and peace is established.

The messianic promises carried such great significance for early Christianity and for the New Testament, above all, because Jesus of Nazareth had received as his most important majestic title the name "Christ," meaning the Messiah, "the anointed one." Because Jesus was the Christ, the messianic promises had to refer to him. The promises about the king of the era of salvation came to be fulfilled in Jesus of Nazareth.

During the history of Christianity, the messianic prophecies have come to be considered by far the most specific and least ambiguous promises of Christ. When one examines the texts of these promises line for line, however, this is certainly not the case, for the divine activity mediated by this Savior-King was not deliverance, but blessing. Nor do the texts contain any indication that suffering had any meaning for the mediator of salvation. Never is forgiveness, the basis for salvation in the New Testament, mentioned. There is almost no connection at all to that which the Gospels report about Jesus, other than that he was also the king of salvation and the anointed one, and the fact that the era of salvation began with his birth. The servant of God passages in Second Isaiah are much closer to Jesus of Nazareth than are the messianic prophecies.

The significance of the messianic prophecies can be recognized in and belong to the broader context of the history of the kingdom in Israel, to which we now turn.

Looking back again over the relation of the message of Old Testament prophecy to Jesus Christ, we conclude that the most substantial part of it does not lie in salvation prophecy, but in the prophecy of judgment.

This means that the prophets' task of announcing God's judgment to the people, which was important in all their activities, also linked them most closely with Christ. This task had made suffering an increasingly important part of the prophets' service, and their suffering, in an apparently fruitless task, is directly linked to the suffering of the servant of God. This, in turn, points ahead to the suffering of Jesus Christ. The prophets' message of salvation, on the other hand, has only an indirect relation to the coming of Christ. Nor do the messianic prophecies in the prophetic books have more than a remote relation to what the New Testament Gospels say about Jesus, the Christ.

Chapter Two

Old Testament Historical Books and Jesus Christ

The Deliverance

In the New Testament, Jesus Christ is proclaimed as Savior. This is true for all the New Testament books, even though they use varying words in describing him. "... there is salvation in no one else ..." was the message announced by the first apostles (Acts 4:12). "Jesus is the Savior" is the statement made about Jesus of Nazareth throughout the entire New Testament. It is the God of salvation who has acted in Jesus Christ. The Old Testament, too, describes a God of salvation who has acted on Israel's behalf. The history of the people of God begins with the saving act of God at the beginning. Their deliverance at the Sea of Reeds (Red Sea) constitutes the basic material of the "historical creed" and is the heart of the Pentateuch.

To what extent this saving act of God continued to be the completely definitive statement about him is seen in the case of Second Isaiah, whose message also promises an act which will deliver the Israelites from their Babylonian exile. Preceding the final deliverance through the deeds, suffering, and resurrection of Jesus Christ, there is a history which leads from Israel's deliverance from elementary need, at the beginning of its national history, to a salvation based on forgiveness, at its end. The experiencing of God as Deliverer or Savior was prerequisite for the New Testament account of God's saving action in Christ. In other words, the New Testament proclamation of Jesus Christ as Deliverer or Savior was not unprecedented: It was preceded by the experience of God as the Savior of his people, an experience which initiated the history of the ancient people of God and affected it until its end.

The historical books of the Old Testament describe the course of what happened between God and his people, from the deliverance at the beginning to the collapse of the nation and the kingdom. When asking to what extent Jesus Christ can be seen as the goal or fulfillment of this history, one must begin with the most elementary principles.

When deliverance is described as it is in the Book of Exodus from beginning to end, we find that it has a certain structure with certain essential ingredients. Deliverance comes about in this way: It is first proclaimed in such a way that a message goes out "to those who wander in darkness." In this message, the Word and the actions of God belong together. In response to the Word comes faith; only if men believe the announcement of deliverance can it become effective for them so that they can escape from captivity. The announcement of deliverance is received from God and passed on to the people by the mediator, the proclaimer of God's message.

In the background of the account of the New Testament Gospels lies this same structure of the salvation event. Though greatly modified because of the changed setting, it is plainly recognizable: When God's saving act in Christ encounters men for whom it has happened, it occurs first through the Word, the message. Only he who believes the Word of deliverance can participate in it. The first result of such faith is that the hearers become followers. The message of deliverance must have one who brings it, the mediator who in this case, however, not only brings the message but makes deliverance a reality through his words, actions, and suffering.

It must be added that the bringer of the message during the exodus had to suffer (Moses' lament), and that in the New Testament the Mediator's suffering takes on decisive meaning for the deliverance he brings.

The deliverance at the beginning (Exodus 1-14) called forth the grateful praise of those who had been saved (Exodus 15), and prompted their readiness to serve this Lord who had saved Israel (Exodus 19-20; Joshua 24). Thus was established the sense of belonging together of God and his people which in the Old Testament is called the Covenant. In the "Covenant

formula" it is expressed in the simplest imaginable
way: "You shall be my people, and I shall be your
God." At its very beginning, this relationship already
was troubled by the apostasy and disobedience of the
people (Exodus 34), and from then on the historical
books tell of continual tension between God's faithful-
ness and Israel's faithlessness. This tension is evident
in the historical documents which contain the history
of Israel. At the center of the Pentateuch stands the
confession of praise of those who have been saved; at
the center of the deuteronomistic history, which contains the books from Deuteronomy (partially) to 2
Kings, is the *confession of guilt* of those who experienced the collapse of the kingdom.

Only by attention to this main historical line is it
possible to say that Christ is the goal of the history of
God's people. The purpose of God's Covenant with his
people is that there be an unbroken reciprocal relation
between them and himself, and the Covenant was established in order that it remain unbroken. To an
ever-increasing extent, however, Israel's history shows
the Covenant being broken by Israel's disobedience.
Finally there comes the announcement that only a new
Covenant can make a future possible for Israel (Jeremiah 31:31-34). This came into existence through
Christ, and the New Testament, too, calls it the "new
Covenant." It is possible to see a relation between
Israel's history and Christ, but it is not possible to
establish a direct connection between Christ and indi-

vidual figures, events, or aspects of this history. The history of the people of God is that of one nation among others, conditioned by the politics of the great powers of the day, and influenced by the cultures, intellectual currents, and religions of the surrounding world.

That this history was a preparation for Christ, and that its goal was Christ's coming can only be sensed in the numerous passages where associations can be seen. Even these passages, however, cannot be thought of as proofs.

The Calling Out and the Following

The early period, before the settlement in the land of Canaan, was considered by many prophets to have been a good time, a time in which, in spite of many shortcomings and deviations, the relation between God and his people was still unbroken. Hence it is understandable that we should find parallels in it to the beginnings of the new people of God.

At the beginning of both the old Covenant and the new Covenant, the first stipulation of deliverance was a "calling out," a call to separateness which resulted in a following. In the New Testament, just as in the Old, history began when a group was called out and became followers. It was a wandering, unsettled group which experienced deliverance from Egypt and found its way through the wilderness; Jesus' disciples were also peri-

patetic and without fixed residence. In both cases the
existence of the followers depended upon who led
them. In each case, to be a follower meant to experience
miracles of deliverance and preservation. In both cases,
too, to obey simply meant to follow: In the community
under way there were as yet no individual commandments and laws. Everything depended on whether the
followers stayed with their leader, abandoning the
group was the *only* sin.

In one case, as in the other, the experiences along the
way determined the relation to God. In neither case
was faith an abstract intellectual process, but rather
something which existed solely in the resolve to follow
and in the carrying out of this resolve. Only an examination of the follower's manner of life can clarify for
us what the Bible means by a confession. Joshua 24 and
John 6:61 ff. show in similar ways the situations out of
which a confession grows. In both cases it is assumed
that long experience preceded the following. The confession is prompted by a question (John 6: "Will you
also go away?"; Joshua 24: "Choose this day whom
you will serve ...") which assumes that it is possible to
abandon the follower's existence. And the single point
of the confession is whether one chooses to remain or
to go away. The confession itself lies in the answer to
a question which is understandable and necessary. The
answer given in the confession confirms following as
existence, just as every authentic confession is an affirmation of following understood as something which
involves man's total existence.

God's Activity in Blessing

All of the parallels mentioned between the history of the first Covenant and Christ have been based on Israel's early period. They have all had to do with the basic facts of salvation summarized in the "historical creed." Israel did not consider what happened after taking possession of the land — that is, after the people had become permanently settled. Following, as a way of life, ceased with the settlement in Canaan; or, more precisely, it existed afterward only as an exceptional manner of life adopted by the prophets. For the people as a whole, the settlement of the land brought a changed form of life and a changed attitude toward God. A new kind of divine activity came to have vital significance, one which was different from that which the people had experienced during their wandering. This was God's constant activity in creating new life, in promoting growth and increase, in short, in that which the Old Testament calls "blessing." The God who delivered now came to be experienced also as the God who blessed. It was a struggle to wrest the power of blessing from the baals, the fertility gods of the land, to overcome the temptation to worship them, and to recognize as Lord of the land and as bestower of blessing the God who had freed them from the Egyptian captivity and led them through the wilderness.

Beginning with the time of settlement, God's activity contained two elements: that which the people had experienced during the exodus from Egypt and the wandering through the wilderness, and that which they were learning as settlers of the land. To the first kind belong elements such as lostness and deliverance, judgment and forgiveness — that divine activity expressed in momentary events. The second element includes his quiet activity in every kind of blessing: earth and body, man's growth and prosperity, plants and animals. To this activity belong soundness and wholeness, and especially the welfare of society, which is peace. While the first of these types of divine activity was restricted primarily to what happened between God and the people, and had, consequently, a historical character in the broad sense of the word, blessing and peace extended beyond the people of God. The Creator blesses his creation, and the era of salvation at the end will be universal and ruled by the language of blessing. Then the peace which ought to pervade the entire creation will be re-established.

The presence of the two themes of deliverance and blessing can be seen in the structure of the Pentateuch. While the books in its middle section, from Exodus to Numbers, are characterized entirely by the redeeming activity of God, the main theological concept in both Genesis and Deuteronomy is that of blessing. The narrative of deliverance is framed by the previous history of how Israel appeared and grew out of the family and the tradition of the Patriarchs, and by Deuteronomy, which looks ahead to a continuing life in the land and promises blessing to the people as long as they are faithful to the God who has saved them.

In addition to these two books, which speak so explicitly of the blessings of God, there is a continuity of God's activity of blessing throughout the entire Old Testament. It is not possible to reduce the theology of the Old Testament to a single continuous salvation history concerned exclusively with deliverance and judgment, the call and the covenant, sin and forgiveness. In addition to that which occurred between God and his people, there is another history which cannot be ignored. In this one, nothing happens except that the stream of life flows on: conception, birth and death, blessing, growth and decline, increase and success, peace and maturation.

The history of worship in Israel provides another illustration of this. That which was special about Israel's worship was its dependence on history. It celebrated the great acts of God; it commemorated the wonders God had performed in the course of Israel's history; it held fast to these earlier events in the face of serious troubles and menaces in the present. Especially characteristic of this aspect of worship was the adding of historical meaning to many of the ancient pagan agricultural and seasonal festivals.

Worship for Israel, however, was always the occasion of God's blessing of his people, a time in which they implored his blessing and thanked him for gifts already received. For Israel blessing remained an essential and necessary ingredient of worship. Only through God's blessing could the nation continue.

At this point, too, we can recognize a parallel to the

Christ event as the New Testament presents it. Although the dominant theological concern of the New Testament is entirely determined by God's single conclusive act of redemption through the suffering, death, and resurrection of Jesus Christ, probably no one would maintain that the entire New Testament is really fully represented in this one theme. It is not accidental that none of the four Gospels confines itself simply to the message of the suffering, death, and resurrection of Jesus, nor that each of them introduces the message with an account of the Jesus who was born, takes part in our life as one who grows and matures, and who promotes life by blessing, healing, preserving, and leading. A whole series of accounts — the healings, the blessing of the children, the blessing of meals, both alone with his disciples and in the community, and many statements such as those about the cares of the day — belong in this context of God's activity of blessing.

There is, however, one special trait of the parables which belongs here and which must be differently interpreted than it ordinarily is. Many parables, in speaking about the coming of God's kingly rule, do so in terms of growing and ripening. They are parables like those about the soil, the seed, the tares among the wheat, the leaven, and the mustard seed. The point of the parable about the four kinds of soil concerns the proclamation of the Word and the acceptance of the proclaimed Word. Proclaiming the Word and accepting or rejecting it, are momentary events which occur in an instant. Yet the action in the parables is constant and gradual, and so does not really match the events and character of their message. If these parables which tell of growth and coming into being are so important to Jesus' message, then a deliberate and paradoxical connection becomes apparent between the momentary and the gradual, a connection calling our attention to the fact that not only the momentary, centered in suffering, death, and resurrection, belongs to the work of Jesus. The continual element which speaks of growth and quiet coming into being also belongs to the coming of God's rule which began with Christ. This second element is closely related to the message of the salvation event in the parables; the exact nature of the relationship, however, is only intimated, never spelled out.

This connection is apparent in Matthew 10 in the commissioning of those whom Jesus sent out: the disciples went out not only to proclaim the message, but also to give a blessing. Similarly, the Acts of the Apostles describes not only the progress of the message, but with it God's activity of blessing, which protects and guides the messengers, heals, and preserves life.

The same connection can be observed in a different manner in the relation between Chapters 1-12 of John's Gospel, dealing with the revelation and issuance of the message, with separation and decision, to Chapters 13-17, which speak about perseverance, about the blessing which Christ gave his disciples as he took leave of them, and about peace. In addition, it should be observed that all the New Testament Epistles contain more than just the message about Christ. They are all framed in greeting and blessing. The blessing includes the congregation's fellowship with the apostle, its preservation and growth, and the peace within it.

Finally, it should be remembered that the God who revealed himself in Christ remains, in the New Testament, the Creator. He who now blesses his people is the Creator who blessed his creatures at the beginning and whose blessing has continued effective through all generations down to the present.

Thankful joy to God at the wonder of the creation, joy in being a creature of God, and blessing, which is the continuing extension of God's creative power, all have their place in that which the Gospels say about Jesus. ("Behold the lilies of the field...!")

However, just as the events at the beginning of the Old Testament found their completion in the Old Testament's description of the goal of history, so the New Testament says that Christ's work will have been completed only at the end of time. In the Book of Revelation, the history of salvation flows once more into the universal history of blessing. That which began with the creation is brought to its conclusion in the final coming of God's kingdom on earth.

Both these basic modes of God's activity, deliverance and blessing, which together constitute the history of the people of God in the Old Testament, are, even though in a different way, at work in the history which began with God's revelation in Christ.

The Kingdom and the Messiah

The kingdom in Israel, the subject of the major part of the historical books (1 Samuel-2 Kings), united in itself the saving and the blessing activity of God. In the hour of its institution, that of the Philistine threat, the kingdom was an instrument of salvation. God granted it to his people to save them from deadly peril at the hands of their enemies. Only in view of this origin can we understand that Jesus' title of Christ signified nothing very different than what was meant by Savior or Deliverer. The kingdom was an institution borrowed from other countries, and Israel adopted an expression of it in which the king was more a bestower of blessing than a savior. Even the title "the anointed one" suggested the constant nature of the king's responsibilities. In the lands which surrounded Israel there was an ancient and well-established theology of kingship. The character of the king as a bestower of blessing had been so clearly imprinted on this theology that even the kingdom in Israel, although quite different in its own beginning and essence, nonetheless adopted a great deal from it.

Nevertheless, the kingdom as an institution never came to real maturity in Israel. It can be said of the history of the kingdom in Israel that it was a history of failure. And so it becomes understandable that the promise which had been given about the kingdom of David (Nathan's promise in 2 Samuel 7) was the beginning of hope for a new and different king, the king of the salvation era. Nathan promised King David that his house — that is, his dynasty — would continue forever. The 89th Psalm, which originated soon after the fall of the Kingdom of Judah and the end of David's dynasty, bears moving witness to what a terrible disappointment the crumbling of Nathan's promise was for the people of God.

For this reason not even the end of the political kingdom could mean that the last word had been spoken. So it was that the expectation of a king of salvation came to life shortly after the Exile in the person of Zerubbabel, a descendant of the house of David who was hailed by the prophets Zechariah and Haggai as the king of the salvation era. But this hope was dashed, for no kingdom came into being. The "No" of God's judgment spoken over the kingdom continued to be decisive.

The promise of a king of salvation lived on. Now, however, that which Isaiah (Chapter 11) and Micah (Chapter 5) said about this future king was radically altered. As we have seen, the messianic prophecies can be understood only in the context of the whole course of the history of the kingdom in Israel. Only in this way could the title of Messiah (anointed king) have been applied to Jesus of Nazareth in spite of his own blunt renunciation of a political kingdom, a refusal repeated throughout the history of the Passion. It was by no means a foregone conclusion that Jesus should receive this title; his activity had decidedly more in common with that of the servant of God. Only when seen in the light of Israel's history can this remarkable fact be explained. The kingdom was an indivisible part of the history of the ancient people of God, and the House of David had received a promise from God which could not fail or remain unfulfilled. What God had wanted to give his people by means of the kingdom did come to fulfillment, though transformed, in the Savior, Jesus the Christ.

As long as it continued, the kingdom had the critical voice of the prophets close at hand; from David to Zedekiah the kingdom and prophecy existed side by side. At no time did any of the prophets, even in their sharpest attacks on the disobedience of the kings, call for a revolution against the king or the abolition of the kingdom. Even when the kings failed, the gift of the kingdom retained its hidden significance. This is shown in the New Testament when Jesus of Nazareth is called the Messiah, even though his activity follows more closely the tradition of the prophets. This must also be understood as the background of Jesus' conversation with Pilate; he answers Pilate's question as to whether he is a king by saying: "I am a king. For this I was born and came into the world, that I should bear witness to the truth." These two statements are contradictory: in the second, the work of a prophet is described, not that of a king. Consequently, this answer becomes intelligible only if Jesus meant to say that the two traditions of God's activity, that of the prophets and that of the kings of Israel, both of which in a sense had failed, had come together and been fulfilled in his own activity and suffering.

Commandments and Laws

A substantial part of the historical books is devoted to "the Law," as it later came to be called. Included are the decalog (the Ten Commandments) and other series of commandments (Exodus 20, Deuteronomy 5, Exodus 34, among others), the Book of the Covenant (Exodus 20-23), the deuteronomic law (Deuteronomy 12-26), the law of holiness (Leviticus 19-26), the law of the priests (Exodus 25–Numbers 10, including the Book of Leviticus) and many single passages. For Paul "the Law" had become synonymous with a process for attaining salvation. It is incorrect to say of the commandments and laws, as they were called in the Old Testament, that they were given as a way of salvation, that is, as a way by which salvation could be attained. Rather, they belong in the context of the people's response to God's saving activity, a response which consists of praise and service. The commandments showed the people how they could serve their God.

Commandments and laws must also be carefully distinguished from one another. In the light of the Old Testament, it is not possible to use the term "Law" for both concepts. A commandment (or prohibition) was given in the second person in the form of direct address, and it was understood as coming directly from God. Commandments are as much a part of God's saving activity in Christ as they were of God's salvation of the ancient people of God. The commandments which Jesus states in the Sermon on the Mount, for instance, belong to this category, as do the exhortations in the letters of the Apostles. The commandment to follow, as it appears in the Gospels, has nothing to do with the "laws." Similarly, the Ten Commandments are not and cannot be classed with them.

The laws differ from the commandments, first of all, in their double form. They establish something which will apply in a given situation: "If someone ... then shall ..." or, "Whoever does this or that shall have this or that done to him." The laws were somewhat similar to what is called statutory law; they are the basic content of legal practice. Statutes are always identified with a certain land and a people, and the legal code of Israel was part of this people's history. Essentially, it was the civil and penal code, similar to those of many other peoples. A comparison of the Book of the Covenant (Exodus 20-23) with the Code of Hammurabi or with other Eastern bodies of law shows that the Israelites had adopted many things in their legal code from their neighbors. That Israel's laws were a part of the history of its people can also be seen in the fact that they changed along with history; when social institutions changed, the laws had to be altered.

What was special about Israel's laws, as seen in the Old Testament, was that they were continually and increasingly being linked with God's activity and with the worship service, being influenced, therefore, by what was happening between God and man. This can be seen in the development from the Book of the Covenant to the deuteronomic law, to the law of holiness (Leviticus 19-26), and, finally, to the law of the priests. Thus, "the Law's" more or less exclusive concern with the relation to God holds true only for the last phase of Israel's history. It was not until this period that the laws became "the Law," with a pronounced theological meaning. Not until the laws had come to be concentrated exclusively on the worship ritual and other aspects of the relation to God did a piety develop which made "the Law" the basis for the entire relation to him. Only by knowing the history of the Law in the Old Testament can we understand what the New Testament says about the Law.

When Paul and John contrast law and grace or law and gospel in an all-decisive antithesis ("... the law was given through Moses; grace and truth came through Jesus Christ," John 1:17), this distinction applies only to the last phase of the history of the Law in the Old Testament, not to its entire history.

Therefore it is a fundamental error, indefensible in the light of a historical interpretation of the Bible, to label the entire Old Testament, or the entire relation to God expressed in the Old Testament, as "the Law," and then set it up in contrast to the New Testament, which, in turn, is made identical with "the Gospel" or "the Gospel of Grace." The history of the ancient people of God begins with a message of salvation, just as a message of deliverance initiates the history of his New Testament people. In the first Covenant, as in the new, the message which grows out of the existence and history of the people of God is clearly that of the grace of God.

What Paul and John meant by "the Law" in the New Testament was the Law which, during the later period, had come to occupy the central position in the relation to God; it had taken on an absolute meaning and had obscured the free and purely gracious act of God's deliverance. Hence it is incorrect to identify Paul's and John's concept of the Law with the use and meaning of the laws valid among the people of Israel around the time of the Exile, or with the laws as they had been understood before that time.

A basic revision of this no longer tenable unhistorical view of the Law is necessary, not only for the sake of clarity within Christian theology, but for the sake of the conversation with Judaism and with Jewish interpreters of the Scriptures.

The History of the People and the Patriarchs

The earliest history, recorded in Genesis 1-11, gains what is perhaps its most important point of relation to Jesus Christ in the fact that in the New Testament (Romans 5:21) Christ is declared to be Adam's counterpart: As through the one, Adam, sin and death came into the world, so through the one man, Christ, came life and justification before God. We shall not consider Paul's specific theological arguments. However, the important thing about this passage is that it associates the work of Jesus Christ with all human beings. This is in harmony with what is said in Genesis 1-11. This is a theme of basic importance: All the works and words of God in the context of the earliest history apply to all humanity and to the world in general. The universalism of the New Testament, which proclaims that the works and words of Christ, together with his suffering and resurrection, happened for all people, is based on what this earliest history says about God. Before the choosing of his people, he was the Creator of the world and of mankind. He blesses man and all life, giving to all living things a vital energy which has retained its force down to the present, and will continue to do so until the end of the world.

Further, the primeval history of the Old Testament establishes that man, a creature of God, finds his decisive limitations in sin, death, and fallibility. The passage cited, Romans 5:12-21, relates the work of Christ to just these critical limitations and proclaims their removal through him. This liberation from man's limitations is at first realized only in the person of Jesus Christ and by faith in him, but it will be revealed to the whole world when he returns at the end of time.

With this, we come to the third manner in which the earliest Old Testament account bears on Christ: primeval history, in telling of the creation of the world and of man, implies that they can come to an end. The origin of the world and of man in the creative activity of God (through the Word of the Creator) includes the possibility of their end, as is illustrated especially in the story of the flood. If, therefore, the work of Jesus Christ is concerned with death and fallibility, then his work must be related to all of man's history. And so that which happened in the "fullness of time" has a bearing on man's history and the history of the world, and will until the end of history. Consequently, that which is said in the Gospels about the end of the world and the return of Christ, as well as that which the rest of the New Testament, in passages such as those in Revelation, says about the end of the world and the return of Christ, is an indispensable part of his work. These basic themes of the New Testament message, which describe an event of cosmic proportions, are to be found already in this earliest Old Testament history.

The relation of the history of the Patriarchs (Genesis 12-50) to Jesus Christ was indirect and distant. It can be studied in three complexes of relationships. The idea of promise, of such significance in the history of the Patriarchs, pointed to the importance of looking toward the future which it shared with the other books of the Bible; the expectant tension between promise and fulfillment was one of the links between the Old and New Testaments. The words of the promise which Abraham received (Genesis 12:1-3), "by you all the families of the earth will bless themselves," are like a bridge which connects universal history (Genesis 1-11) with the history of Israel's election (Genesis 12). The promises given first to the Patriarchs and then to the people of Israel were to remain open to fulfillment until they again converged on the universal horizon hinted at from the beginning (for example, John 3:16). Therefore this basic orientation toward the future characterized all of the people of God.

The form of society which marked the life of the Patriarchs was the family or kinship. The forms of life we meet in the history of the Patriarchs are those of a prenational existence. The New Testament congregation was a social structure existing within the nation and including really only the Lord and his disciples; moreover, the disciples are all brothers. The social structure of the Christian church or congregation is *related* more closely to the family than to any other institution, but until now it has *resembled* more closely the state than the family. What the family social structure, which the Bible intended to be the form of the church, could mean for our world will not be clear until a future ecumenical church has freed itself from forms inherited from the medieval. To establish the structure the Bible intended for the Christian church, it is important that the basic structures of the family, especially as they are found in the history of the Patriarchs, be rediscovered. Particularly vital would be to determine exactly what is meant in the Bible by "brother" and by being a brother.

Finally, it is this idea of brotherhood, as developed in the history of the Patriarchs, which provides an important indication of the unity of the Bible. At the climax of the story of Joseph it is hinted that one brother can suffer (by becoming a slave) for another, so that society as a whole may remain intact or become sound once more (Genesis 44:18-34). This passage is not to be understood as a prophecy of Christ or anything similar. Taken in the context of the history of the Patriarchs, it is a hint that "being a brother," which is pregnant with an abundance of possible ways of acting in human situations, can include even this last possibility: that a brother voluntarily (see Philippians 2) steps before a condemned society, ready to suffer personally the punishment deserved by others. There is, then, a significant connection, meaningful from the perspective of history, between the brother's words, spoken to those in power, in which he declares his readiness to suffer in his brother's stead, and the servant of God passage in Isaiah 53, in which "the brothers" realize that someone has suffered in their place.

Chapter Three

Response of God's People and Jesus Christ

Everything which happened in Israel between God and man was an event in the form of dialogue. In response to a lament from the depths of distress and desperation came God's help; then followed, as Israel's answer to the act of deliverance, joyful praise to God.

The Old Testament reports both the saving acts of God and Israel's response to them. It is for this reason that complaint and praise to God, the two principal types of material in the Psalter, are also found repeatedly in the historical books. Beginning with the psalm of praise of the people freed from Egypt, in Exodus 15, down through the numerous psalms in 1 and 2 Chronicles, complaint and praise comprise a substantial part of Old Testament history.

It is significant, therefore, to investigate the connection between the Psalms and Jesus Christ.

Christ and the Complaint of His People

Early Christianity's use of the 22nd Psalm to describe Jesus' sufferings, even in such details as his crying out on the cross (Psalm 22:1), was more than a casual quotation of Scripture. The accumulation of passages from this one psalm (v. 2: Matthew 27:46, Mark 15:34; v. 8: Mark 27:39, Mark 15:29; v. 9: Matthew 27:43; v. 16: John 19:28; v. 19: Matthew 27:35, John 19:23-24) shows that early Christianity assumed that it had a special relation to Christ. At one time, this relation was understood as a foretelling of Christ, "one of the divinely ordained prefigurations," as a Psalm commentator of the last century put it. However, Psalm 22 is not soothsaying but a prayer, and must be taken seriously as such down to its very last word. Thus, if this psalm refers to Christ, it can do so only as a prayer.

At this point we can gain an important insight into the New Testament's understanding of the resurrection. It had always been assumed that the narrative of Christ's suffering and death was complete and self-sufficient, and that the account of the resurrection was also independent and complete in itself. Seen from an Old Testament standpoint, this is incorrect; the accounts of the resurrection of Christ cannot be considered or treated apart from the Passion history, as the use of Psalm 22 to describe the whole story indicates. This is further confirmed by Isaiah 53, which also presents the suffering, death, and glorification of the servant of God as unquestionably unified and complete.

The 22nd Psalm belongs to the class of psalms called "laments of the individual." Within this class there is a special group, "the complaint of the mediator," that is, the lament of the one suffering under the heavy load of his responsibility to stand between God and man. Especially clear examples are the complaints of Moses (for example, Exodus 5:22), of Joshua (7:7-9), Elijah (1 Kings 19), the laments of Jeremiah (11-20), and the servants of God passages (Isaiah 49:1-6; 50:4-9). The complaints of those who mediated between God and the people show that suffering belonged in a special degree to their office.

Here we need to look again at that which was previously said about the nature of the saving event. It was said that an essential part in it is played by the mediator, that is, the one who brings the announcement of deliverance to those in distress. As the complaints of Moses show, suffering in his day already was part of the mediator's task.

When it is further noted that Jeremiah's complaints correspond closely in language and structure to the complaints of the individual in the Psalms, that they are, in fact, psalms of complaint modified to fit the prophet's (the mediator's) situation, then it becomes clear that there is a profound connection between the complaint of the mediator, as he exercises his office among the people of God, and the life and suffering of the same people. The mediator is, in fact, one of these people, one of the nameless sufferers.

The use of the 22nd Psalm in connection with

Christ's suffering and death points to the mystery of
the incarnation; conversely, the incarnation can be
understood only in the context of the entire history
of God and his people. If there are any themes in the
Old Testament which lead to Christ, the lament of
the mediator is one of them. And yet, the mediator's
complaint is essentially the lament of man in his suffering and trouble, in his human existence. This is a
lament which Christ took upon himself.

The Praise of God

The psalms or hymns of praise focus decisively upon
praise of God: He is praised for his majesty and good-
ness, but not in such a way as to imply that these are
unchangeable qualities. God is wonderful because in
his majesty he turns to men in kindness, especially to
those who are suffering. Out of his exaltation he looks
down into our insignificance.

> Who is like the Lord our God,
>   who is seated on high,
> who looks far down
>   upon the heavens and the earth?
> (Psalm 113:5 f.)

This astonished joy at God's inclining to the depths
of human suffering and guilt pervades all of Israel's
psalms of praise.

This is also the explanation given in the New Testament for Jesus Christ's mission, for his coming into
the world: God had turned in mercy to his people:

"Blessed be the Lord God of Israel, for he has visited and redeemed his people."   (Luke 1:68)

All of the numerous quotations from the Psalms in Chapters 1 and 2 of Luke sound this same note, and it also appears often in the rest of the New Testament (for example, John 3:16). When we compare the praise-of-God motif in the Psalms with praise of God in the Christian church, the similarity becomes even more striking. In the church, praise of God is most typically expressed in the Christmas carols, which are full of the theme of God's inclining to the depths of human sorrow. In the incarnation God's willingness to stoop to the lowest level of man's need found its perfect expression:

Gott gibt, unserm Leid zu wehren, seinen Sohn aus dem Thron seiner Macht und Ehren.

The statement is often made that the Father to whom Jesus prayed was the God of the Old Testament. This does not say a great deal, however, unless it is explained why this is so. To be theologically significant, this statement would have to say that the God who was praised by Israel is the God who looks down into the depths of human grief to help those who are suffering. It would have to be added, also, that Christianity understands the incarnation to be the self-revelation of this God. The distinctive nature of God's divinity is his saving activity, which is best illuminated in Israel's praise: "He who has his dwelling on high — he who sees into the depths." This praise says the same thing about the God of Israel that the historical creed

does in another manner. God, as Deliverer, encountered
Israel at the beginning of its history and his final self-
revelation in Jesus Christ again showed him to be the
Deliverer.

The narrative praise of God (generally called psalms
of thanksgiving) differs from the descriptive praise in
that it tells of a specific act of deliverance which the
psalmist has just experienced. The narrative psalm of
praise has an especially well established structure. The
psalmist reports his experience with God's saving intervention in a certain series of events. A declaration (for
example, "I will extol thee ..."), and an introductory
summation are followed by a backward glance at the
trouble; then comes the main body of the report of
deliverance, stated in three parts: I cried out — he heard
me — he saved me. In the final part, the promise to
praise God is renewed, and the psalm closes with praise
of God. This structure can be found, for example, in
Psalms 18, 30, 40, and 66:13-20. We find a similar pat-
tern in the words of praise in the preamble of Luke's
Gospel (1:68-75 and 2:29-32), in which God is praised
for his conclusive act of deliverance.

Beyond this, the structure of the Book of Romans, in
which deliverance through Christ is the central theme,
shows a clear similarity to the structure of the narrative
psalm of praise. After the declaration (1:14 ff.) comes
the introductory summation (1:16 ff.), the backward
glance at the trouble (1:18-3:20), and the report of
deliverance (3:21-8:39), in which the three-part organization "I cried out — he heard me — he saved me" can

still be detected in Chapter 7. The renewed vow of praise is sounded in 12:1 ff. (the beginning of the admonitions), and the last chapter ends with praise to God (16:25-27).

Once more, however, the similarity can best be observed in the hymns of the Christian church. The hymn, "Sing Praise to God Who Reigns Above," by Johann Jakob Schütz, employs the narrative praise of the psalmist almost literally to express the Christian experience, and Luther's Reformation hymn, "Dear Christians, One and All, Rejoice," parallels — though probably not consciously — the structure of the narrative psalm of praise in each of its parts, from the declaration and introductory summation in the first stanza, through the retrospect of the trouble in stanzas two and three, the report of deliverance in stanzas four through nine, to its tenth and last stanza, which ends by praising God.

In the narrative psalm of praise, the one who has been delivered proclaims God's mighty acts. So do the messengers of Jesus Christ (Acts 2:11). In the sending of the Son, God's saving acts found their fulfillment.

The Petition Against the Enemies

The two basic ways of calling on God shown in the Psalms are praise of him and complaint to him. On the basis of these two ways alone, an attempt has been made to demonstrate the Old Testament's connection with Jesus Christ. If this relationship can be clearly shown in these types of Old Testament literature, it may also be possible to show how the coming of Christ changed what takes place between God and man in the form of complaint or lament.

It has already been said that Christ accepted and took upon himself the lament of those who had suffered to the point of being forsaken by God. In the Old Testament, prayers to God directed against enemies belonged to the category of lament. This type is also found in the complaint of the mediator, especially in the Lamentation of Jeremiah. In the Old Testament the request for God's intervention against enemies was necessary because, according to its teaching, everything which could happen between God and men had to happen on this side of the grave. It had to be clear in this life which side God was on, for he could act in behalf of a supplicant only by acting against his enemy.

This situation, however, changed when Christ broke through the boundary of death by his suffering, death, and resurrection. Because God showed himself to be on the side of the one who was defeated and executed, even death became a positive action of God. The Gospels express this changed situation through their account of Jesus' intercession on the cross for his enemies. The plea for God's action against a man's enemies became unnecessary; it was erased from the Christian's prayer by Christ's prayer for his enemies.

This is only one example of how Christ's taking on himself a situation from the Old Testament could lead to a profound change in what the Old Testament says.

Chapter Four

Literature of Wisdom and Jesus Christ

Aside from the Psalms, the principal content of the third part of the Old Testament canon is the literature of wisdom (Proverbs, parts of Job, Ecclesiastes, and individual passages in other books).

The reason why the wisdom literature belongs in the canon, or why it was taken into it, is not immediately apparent. For one thing, the wisdom literature has nothing to do with history, has no place in the history of God and his people, and makes practically no reference to this history. Also, the original body of this literature is practical, worldly wisdom which has nothing to do with what happens between God and man. What it does say about God's activity is so general that the same statements could as well have been made about other religions. The statements are similar to those which were usual during the era of Rationalism. The true and specifically godly wisdom was not added until later.

It seems probable that the "wisdom" books were made part of the canon for the sake of this pious God-related wisdom. ("The fear of the Lord is the beginning of wisdom.") Yet this explanation is not altogether satisfactory in view of the important role played in Proverbs and Ecclesiastes by a kind of simply secular wisdom which is totally unrelated to God and his works.

The theological justification of the "wisdom literature," its anchoring in the works of God, must be accomplished in a different way. In the Old Testament, maturity cannot be separated from wisdom which originated and ripened in experience. Consequently, age and wisdom belong together and wise counsel comes from experienced men. Wise exhortation was that which the elders gave to the young, a fact which accounts for the form of address so common in the wisdom literature: "My son...." This implied that the process of growth and maturation was an essential prerequisite for wisdom.

This process of growing and ripening was understood in the Old Testament to be the fruit of God's blessing, and blessing is the power to grow. Because in the Old Testament man was understood in his wholeness, this power to grow affected all of him, body, soul, and spirit, in all his possibilities and capacities. The power of this blessing includes even that which is said as a result of this process of growth and maturing — that is, the words of wisdom which arise from God's power to bless and are intended, through comparison and warning and through its statements of experience and exhortation, to help man master and improve his life. Seen in this way, it becomes understandable, even significant, that the words of wisdom of other peoples could have been incorporated into the books of wisdom in the Old Testament (for example, Proverbs 30-31). God's power to bless was not limited to the people of Israel.

In investigating the relation of the Old Testament wisdom literature to Jesus Christ, a beginning can be made with the account of the twelve-year-old Jesus in the temple. The story ends with: "And Jesus increased in wisdom and stature, and in favor with God and man" (Luke 2:41-52). Here is meant the power of blessing which affects the whole person. By putting this story and this statement at the end of the introduction to his Gospel, Luke intends to say that Jesus participated in the process of growth and maturation, just as every man does, and that wisdom had a share in his speech and his message. The words of Jesus are not to be understood as strictly analogous to the words of a prophet, that is, as words which he simply received and passed on. The word of wisdom which had grown and matured also contributed to Jesus' message, and this participation of wisdom in his proclamation was a consequence of the incarnation.

The facts of the matter are unequivocal and can easily be established by attention to Jesus' message as it is presented in the synoptic (the first three) Gospels. The "wisdom" elements appear in many kinds of contexts: in exhortations, in controversies, in the instruction of the disciples, and, above all, in the parables. In Proverbs, the brief comparison or explained parable is an important ingredient of the wisdom address or words of wisdom. In his parables Jesus blends this device with his message of the coming kingdom. This has a meaning for his teaching which has not yet received the attention it deserves. The coming of the kingdom of God, the proclamation of the good news, the invitation to accept this message — all these are momentary events which belong in the context of the history of the people of God. But the words of wisdom in the form of the parables constitute a pronounced counterpoint to momentary events. The content of Jesus' wisdom address corresponds to its parable form and is a further indication of its relation to the Old Testament. It speaks of growing, increasing, and ripening, of the quiet, unobtrusive process of becoming and changing. Here I refer again to what was said in the New Testament about the importance of blessing.

Just as saving and blessing activities are combined in the work of Jesus of Nazareth, so are two corresponding ways of speaking about God's actions combined in his message. Side by side with his proclamation of the coming of the kingdom of God and his call to faith which accompanied it, he used another kind of language which grew entirely out of common human experience. This way of talking, which had matured in close contact with human beings, made up an appreciable part of Jesus' message. The Old Testament's wisdom passages had grown out of Israel's daily experience and matured through its coexistence with other peoples; they certainly did not originate exclusively with Israel. In the same way, Jesus' parables and the other wisdom passages which belong to his message contain a substantial element of that which is an inseparable part of his message.

Seen in this way, there is also a clear and plainly demonstrable relation between the wisdom literature of the Old Testament and Jesus Christ.

Fulfillment of the Promise

Near the beginning of the Gospel of Luke (4:16-21) we are told how Jesus, during a visit to the synagogue in Nazareth, asked for the scroll of the prophet Isaiah, read aloud a passage from it (Isaiah 61:1-2), closed the scroll and said, "Today this scripture has been fulfilled in your hearing." This story provides a good example of what the Old Testament meant to Jesus himself.

The account tells us that Jesus went to the synagogue on the Sabbath, as he was accustomed to do. In doing so, he chose to participate in the existing order of things. The statement he made, "Today . . . has been fulfilled . . . ," was said during a worship service which he had not instituted and within a liturgical framework which had existed long before his birth.

After the destruction of the temple during the Babylonian Exile, an entirely new type of worship service, with Scripture as the central factor, appeared in Israel. The Word of God went out to the congregation, and the congregation answered, directing its response to

75

God in confession, prayer, and psalms. The temple ritual was closed to non-Jews, but the service in the synagogue was open to all, and the movement to make proselytes went out from the synagogue, not from the temple.

The worship service of early Christianity adopted from the synagogue its two principal elements: proclamation of God's Word to the people, and the people's response in prayer and praise. The Christian congregation established no new kind of worship. The nature and history of Christian worship can be explained and understood only in the light of this earlier history of worship in the synagogue.

The heart of the worship service in the synagogue was the reading of the Scriptures from the Old Testament. This kind of worship could come into existence in Israel only because there the Word of God, in both its written and spoken form, had such decisive importance. The meaning of the Bible for the Christian worship service is based on the importance of the Word of God among the ancient people of God. Only by being joined to the Old Testament, the Bible accepted at that time in both the synagogue and by the early Christians, did the New Testament become a part of the Bible. The Christian congregation learned from the Old Testament what the Bible means: the Word of God, received through tradition and given current meaning in the worship service.

In Luke 4:16-21 we find the relation of the Old

Testament to the New Testament to be that of a promise which was fulfilled in Christ. It is possible to understand this fulfillment as meaning that "now that the light has come, everything which had come before is overshadowed," or as "that which is provisional, having now been confirmed in its provisional nature, loses its meaning for those who enjoy the light of the fulfillment." However plausible this may sound, and however much it may seem to agree with many New Testament passages, it is not the relation between promise and fulfillment intended in the Bible. To divorce promise as event, the living process by which the promise was given, from that which was promised, to insist on having the fulfillment without the promise — means that promise is no longer promise. This can be seen in the example of the promise of the land in the Old Testament. The promise was fulfilled; Israel received the land "flowing with milk and honey," and settled in it. That did not mean, however, that it stopped being the promised land. The promise did not lose its meaning because the fulfillment had come. As long as Israel lived in the land, it continued to comprehend the gift of the land entirely in relation to the promise. It continued to be the land which once had been promised to the Patriarchs, for only in this way could it continue to be received as a new gift from the hand of God.

The same is true of that promise of which Christ was the fulfillment. As we have seen, the promise is

closely intertwined with the history which led to Christ.
If one separates this history of the promise from its
fulfillment, then Christ and his work cease to be fulfillment. Only when the events of the promise are given
their due and when the Old Testament is given significance is it possible to accept the work of Jesus
Christ as the fulfillment of the promises and of the
history of the promise. The fulfillment can only then
be recognized as such when the story is told of how
the promise was given.

The relation of the Old Testament to the New Testament can, therefore, no longer be viewed in such a
way as to say that the Old Testament contains that
which is promised, and the New Testament that which
is fulfilled. Rather, one must say that the Old Testament contains the history of the promise fulfilled in the
New Testament. Promise and fulfillment constitute
an integral event which is reported in both the Old
and New Testaments of the Bible.

The relationship of promise and fulfillment is fundamental and decisive, not only for the understanding
of the relationship of the Old Testament to Jesus Christ,
but of the Testaments to one another.

Yet it is not possible to sum up everything in the
relation of the Old Testament to Christ under the
single idea of promise and fulfillment. In fact, it is
not possible to equate this relationship with any one
idea, for it is essentially a historical relationship. God
accompanied his people on a journey which led from

Abraham and to the exodus from Egypt to Christ. What happened along the way is a diverse, many-sided, changing process. In the same way, the relation of the Old Testament to Jesus Christ is diverse, many-sided, and changing (Hebrews 1:1).

The abundance and variety of forms in which we see this relationship result only partly from its having taken place as a lengthy process within history, with all the transformations which this implies. It is also founded on the nature of the Old Testament itself, which contains such diverse ingredients as books of history, prophecy, psalms, and wisdom. Only when we take seriously each of these categories, with all the different elements each contains, do the richness and variety of these relationships reveal themselves fully. Only through this many-sided preparatory history, which embraces all creation and human existence, does the Gospel of Jesus, the Christ, receive the background against which its fullness and richness become comprehensible for our day.

In conclusion, it should be said that this relationship of the Old Testament to Jesus Christ is so productive that it certainly cannot be grasped by any one generation. Thus, the purpose of what has been said here is simply to help see that further questions be asked, erroneous ideas be corrected, and new and different insights be gained. This work will have been successful if it stimulates someone to move forward beyond traditional and restricting thought patterns and terminology into the unsuspected and profound relationships between the Old Testament and Jesus Christ. Only when the whole message of Christ is rooted in the Old Testament can it be understood and attract listeners in our day.